Lawn care: 51 Tips for Taking Care of Your Lawn

By Timothy Barkley

Table of Contents

Introduction

What is the first thing pops up in your mind when you hear about lawn care? Oh My God! It is literally impossible for a person to take care of such a big area alone. In our super busy life the mere thought of cleaning the house scares us to death, which is very small place compared to a lawn. Well, in that case I would say a house cannot take care of itself, but the nature can. All you need to do is to give a little hand.

Unlike houses and streets, natural places like lawns have a repair system of their own. Lawns have their own alarm system to warn you about the problems they are facing and they also have different ways to deal with it. However, there may come some times when their automatic repair and maintenance system may not be enough to keep your lawn beautiful, luscious and green look. You need to listen and take necessary actions to combat the issues.

Worried, how are you going to do this since you do not have the expertise? You don't need to, nor do you need to call professionals and splash your hard-earned cash. Just read through the tips and suggestions given in this book, try to follow them and leave everything to the nature itself. Only you know your lawn well and in your hand only your lawn can receive the best care and maintenance.

Chapter 1- Background of your Lawns and Care

History

Past records state that the idea of lawn originated from the early medieval times based on the concept of enclosed grass fields that were distinctively used for grazing livestock, and was separated from the ones reserved for agricultural purposes. The word "laune" was first verified in 1540 and was related to the Celtic Brythonic term laun, meaning sacred enclosure for worship.

Since the middle ages, the aristocracy in northern Europe was behind the huge popularity of lawns till now. Earlier, people could not always distinguish pasture fields from lawns. Many speculations revealed that to some citizen, lawns were considered to be a part of cultural kinship. In the north, the maritime Western Europe's damp and mushy climate favored the growth and management of lawns. Until the modern-day influence took over, lawns could not make its place as a part of gardens in other cultures and places of the world.

In 1830 prior to the invention of mowing machines, people used to manage their lawns in different ways. They have counted as and the pompous element of manor houses and wealthy estates. In some places, maintaining lawns required labor-intensive work of trimming and mowing. Most of the time, lawns were used as pasture lands and were maintained through grazing animals, like sheep and other livestock. Sheep, rabbits or horses used to graze some areas of the land regularly for many days. These areas eventually used to look like the modern day tight-prairie, low lawns.

This was the original essence of the term "lawn". Still today in many forest regions where excessive grazing happens, patches of semi-natural lawns can be noticed. For instance, this kind of overgrazed lands is commonly seen in the New Forest England and those are known as lawns. One of such lawns is Balmer Lawn. Lawns like today's ones first seen in England and France in the 1700s when the garden of Versailles was designed by André Le Nôtre which had a small zone of grass, known as the "green carpet".

Early Lawns in England

In the 18th or 19th century, the lawns and the gardens became a place of recreation, strolling or social gatherings. During that time, the lawns were decorated with varieties of meadow plants. Chamomile was the most favorite of all. Early 17th century was the starting era of Jacobean gardening. During this month, the birth of "English" lawn took place. By the end of this epoch, English lawn had earned its fame as the symbol of elite and aristocracy. This was a medium to let people know that owner could keep land for beautification and social gathering, and not for harvest and construction.

At the beginning of 18th century, the golden age of landscape gardening for the gentry started, under the supervision of Lancelot "Capability" Brown and William Kent. They modified the traditional look of English landscape garden by giving a touch of nature and romantic setting for the rich Englishmen. Brown is still renowned as the "England's best gardener" who design over 170 parks, some of which still exist. His influence and reputation were so prodigious that the additions and that his predecessors William Kent and Charles Bridgeman made were overseen most of the time.

Brown's art still sustains at Croome Court (the place where he also planned the house), Warwick Castle, Harewood House, Blenheim Palace, Milton Abbey, Bowood House, few places in Kew Gardens and several other places. His style of creating smooth heaving lawns which ran impeccably to the meadow house, belts, clamps, and scattering of trees and his twisting lakes formed by unnoticeably stemming small rivers, were a new fashion within the English landscape. In other words, his designs were "gardenless" arrangement of landscape gardening, which swept away almost all the miscellanies of old patterned trends. The art that his designs of landscapes possessed were fundamentally untraditional from the ones that were replaced.

The so-called "English style" of parkland first became popular across Ireland and Britain, and next across Europe. One of the examples is "garden à la française" which was overtaken by the "French landscape garden".

As the time passed by, the concept of lawn in England gradually started to mean an area of garden which is covered with grass and very deeply mowed. During the late 18th century in America, rich families also were seen to copy the style of English landscapes. Around 1780 in North America, the Shaker community was the first to initiate the industrial production of high-quality grass seed. They also built several nurseries and kernel companies in Philadelphia. The abundant availability of these grasses caused these to be supplied for livestock, as well as, residential areas and parks.

Chapter 2- Characterisation of Plants in Lawns

People like to plant many different types of grasses. The choice depends on the climate and the purpose of usage. Fields on which active sports are played are covered with coarse grasses, whereas finer grasses are ideal for decorative lawns for their artistic values. Some grasses are well adapted to continental and tropical climates with hotter summers. Others are suited to oceanic climates with colder summers. Most of the time, a combination of low plant types and grass is used to make a stronger lawn. In this way, one type of plant can withstand colder weathers while the other type of plant can survive in the hotter seasons. This combination is taken one step forward by a breed of grass that can produce cultivars. The cultivar is a cross-breed of two different types of grass and intends to mix certain features taken from each breed of grass. As a result, a new breed is invented which is specialized and well suited to a specific environment, like a low nutrient, low water, and low light.

It is not necessary that lawns must always be covered with green grass and exceptions have been seen in several cases. Other lawn-like garden areas can also use plants including ground covers, sedges, wildflowers and low herbs on which you can easily walk without destroying it completely.

There are numerous variations of grasses and imitations of grass plants that can be utilized in lawns. These plants are well adapted to specific conditions of irritation, precipitation, seasonal temperatures and tolerances from sun and shade. Botanists and hybridizers of plants are constantly trying to make and look for improved varieties of the fundamental species and new ones. These must be economical and environmentally very sustainable with less need for water, fertilizer, pest, treatments from diseases and maintenance. Based on these attributes, grasses can be divided into three categories, they are:

Summer Grasses

Grasses in hot or warm climates only begin to grow only at temperatures above 10 °C (50 °F), and grow at the fastest rate at temperatures between 25 °C (77 °F) and 35 °C (95 °F). These have one very long period of growth over the summer and spring (Huxley 1992). Often they become quiescent in colder months developing shades of tan and brown. Several types of grasses of warm climates are extremely drought tolerant and is very resistive against very high summer temperatures. However, most of the southern ecotype grasses of warm climate can be destroyed at temperatures below −15 °C (5 °F). The northern diversities, like blue grama and buffalo grass, are very resilient to 45 °C (113 °F).

- Buffalograss (drought tolerant)
- Grama grass
- St. Augustine grass
- Bahiagrass (Paspalum)
- Centipedegrass (Eremachloa)
- Carpetgrass (Axonopus)
- Zoysiagrass (Zoysia spp.)
- Bermudagrass (Cynodon spp.)

Winter Grasses

Grasses in cold seasons begin to grow at 5 °C (41 °F), and the rate of their growth reach the highest at temperatures between 10 °C (50 °F) and 25 °C (77 °F), in climates that have moderately cool/mild summers, with two periods of fast growth in the autumn and spring. In extremely cold weather, these can retain their colors and normally growth very thick somewhat like carpets with a little straw.

- *Native plant regional choices (for taller lawns):*
    - Tufted hair grass (Deschampsia spp.)
    - Cluster fescue (Festuca paradox spp.)
    - Red fescues (Festuca Rubra)
    - Feather reed grass (Calamagrostis spp.)
- *Typical choices:*
    - Ryegrasses (Lolium spp.)
    - Fescues (Festuca spp., hybrids, and cultivars)
    - Bluegrass (Poa spp.)
    - Bentgrass (Agrostis spp.)

Alternative to Ground Cover

Some people like to cover their lawns with low ground creepers, like creeping jenny, creeping thyme, purple flowering Mazus, creeping sedums, grey Dymondia, chamomile and Lippia. You can also choose from other lawn alternatives, such as kitchen gardens, meadows, butterfly gardens, rain gardens, tapestry lawn, native plant habitat gardens, paved Spanish courtyard, patio gardens and drought tolerant xeriscape. In traditional cottage or wildlife gardens, shrubs and trees growth very close to the surface of lawns provide habitat for some birds.

Alternatives to Grass

In the horticulture industry, cultivars and carex species are known as 'sedge' alternatives for 'grass' in mowed garden meadows and lawns. Both of these grow very low and are ornamental cultivars and native species that spreads and are used for long lasting landscaping as drought tolerant and low maintenance grass replacements for garden meadows and lawns. These are used in gardens, for the restoration of wildland projects and natural landscaping for the 'user-friendly' zones. In Los Angeles, J. Paul Getty Museum incorporated Carex PAE gracilise (dune sedge) and Carex Pansa (meadow sedge) generously in the Sculpture gardens. Names of some of the lower sedges include:

- C. tumulicola (foothill sedge) (cultivar 'Santa Cruz Mnts. selection')
- C. uncifolia (ruby sedge)
- Carex caryophyllene (cultivar 'The Beatles')
- C. divulsa (Berkeley sedge)
- C. pansa (meadow sedge)
- C. praegracilis (dune sedge)
- C. subfusca (mountain sedge)
- C. glauca (blue sedge) (syn. C. flacca)

Chapter 3- 51 Tips for Taking Care of Lawn

Several types of problems may cause damage to your beautiful lawn for which it may not look lively and vibrant. There is nothing to worry about. Every problem has a solution. Even dead looking lawn can be restored to its healthy state if proper steps are taken. Below are given 51 tips of how to take care of your lawn properly and maintain its good health.

1. Weedkiller for Lawn Weeds

Common lawn weeds, such as the blue-flowered speedwell, daisies, lesser trefoil, dandelion, yarrow, buttercups, parsley-piert and black medick, need to be treated in time. Otherwise, these will eventually spread to compete against the grass for food, light and space. So, your grass will not look so healthy. In this case, use a good quality weedkiller to kill the weeds without damaging the grass.

2. Drench Lawn with Di-hydrogen Monoxide

Sometimes applying chemicals and pesticides can impose long-term effect on your lawn. Your plants and flowers may get affected. That is why is always recommended to use as less chemicals as possible. However, weeds can completely damage your lawn and so you need to take proper action against it. One safe and easy homemade solution is that you boil a big pot of Di-hydrogen Monoxide on the stove and pour it over the stems and leaves of the weeds. This will kill the weeds effectively without harming your lawn.

3. Improve Drainage System

Spring and autumn are the most favorable seasons for lawn moss to grow. The moss mostly appear in shady places, or if you have a faulty drainage system. You can solve this problem by applying a good moss killer; however you must improve your drainage system to keep your lawn moss free.

4. Encourage Overseeding

It is a very good idea to improve the vigour of the lawn by overseeding it with a mixture of grass and seed. This method is particularly suited for shaded areas. Also, add lime to the soil to encourage more growth of grass.

5. Sweep Off Worm Casts

In autumn, your lawn may suffer from a common issue called "worm casts". Squashing these casts will not solve this problem; you are rather making ideal seed beds for weed seeds with the squashed worm casts. The ideal solution is when they appear, you should let them become fully dry and then sweep these off from the lawn with a stiff broom brush before you mow the lawn.

6. Vinegar to the Rescue

A splash of vinegar can be an excellent homemade solution against different types of worms. The solution works as an excellent weed killer too as it causes the moisture being released from whichever organism it touches. Since earthworms need moisture to breathe in, the acidity of vinegar will result in moisture to leave their bodies, and hence cause their death.

7. Scarify the Thatches

Lawn thatch is nothing but a layer of dead and organic stuff at soil level. Thatch is a very bad thing for your lawn. It can prevent water from seeping through the soil surface and can make your lawn more prone to diseases. The solution to this problem is to rack out the thatches with a scarifier or a rake in early spring in around September.

8. Aerate the Soil Core

Let the core of the soil in your lawn aerate properly. This is an important factor to prevent and maintain thatch control. Microbial activity can be increased and thatch can be broken down if regular core aeration is practiced as this improves the air circulation into the soil and prevent compaction. Thatches can also be removed physically with soil aeration.

9. Feed Nutrition to the Grass

Pale colored grass indicated malnutrition due to inadequate amount of food or imbalanced diet supplied to the plant. This usually happens when the plants use up all the available nutrients from the soil. In this case, replace the lost nutrients in the soil by adding supplementary food in the soil.

10. Water Sufficiently to Prevent Browning

Some types of grass and plants have roots that grow deep into the soil. In that case, sufficient amount of watering is needed frequently. Otherwise, the plants may become dry and will start to dry and wilt. The leaves will break and eventually will become susceptible to wear and tear by strong winds. Watering also maintains the optimum temperature of the plant enzymes to function properly.

11. Fungicides for the Lawn Circles

Fairy rings appear in your lawn due to the formation of fungus. Initially, the grass in the circle will look greener due to presence of more decaying organic matter in the circle that provides it with more moisture. As fungus grows, it will starve the roots of nutrients and moisture. Treat this by using fungicide. Watering may worsen the issue in this case.

12. Prevent Over-shaving the Grass

Shaving the lawn excessively until the land becomes bare is not a good idea. The bare patches can easily be effected by moss and weeds. You can easily solve this issue by filling in hollows with top soil or lawn soil, and trim the grass to a minimum of few centimeters in length. Grass seeds or a mixture of grass seed patches can be utilized to reseed the bare patches.

13. Keep Your Dog Out of Lawn

The problem of scalped patches is commonly seen in the grass of the lawn. Bare patches can sometimes be caused by your dog. They can destroy the grass and the soil while digging holes to hide their bones. In this situation, you can purchase specialised blends of tolerant seeds and grass along with neutralizers.

14. No Growth of Grass under a Tree

If you are living in the northern climates, you can consider planting fine shade-tolerant fescue grass for your lawn. For southern climates, you can try planting tall fescue grass.

15. No Growth of Grass on a Slope

Deep watering might be of use if the slope is dry, hot or more regular. If you cannot plant grass, then you can try placing sod or planting a professional "hydroseed". These are seeds of plants that are encapsulated inside a special material which prevents them from getting dried up.

16. Weeds Overrun the Lawn

During the fall and spring season, apply herbicides. It is recommended that you apply in both the seasons as with each application, different types of weeds are killed. For severe kind of issue, the remedy may not respond in 1 or 2 years. In that case, it is better to kill your lawn completely using a non-selective herbicide and then replant to decorate.

17. Bare Patches on Lawn

You can try reseeding the bare patches. In early fall and in spring, scrape off the bare patch using a ground rake and sprinkle over some grass seed. Make marks around the areas with sticks and strings, and gently pour water. For the next few weeks, keep the area moist and water it daily if needed. If the issue is high traffic, it is a good idea to make a path or patio surface.

18. Weblike Threads and Brown Spots in Lawn

In early spring, Fusarium patches can create 2 to 12-inch wide web like threads in thatch or brown spots and also grass in early spring can be seen. You should apply fungicide in early fall, improve the drainage system, and try to lessen fertilization and shade.

19. Bleached Dots or Grey Spots in Lawn

Dollar spot can cause a lot of such kind of spots to appear in your lawn. Smaller spots may merge together into larger ones and straw-coloured areas. On the other hand, cobweb-like growth can also be seen with morning dew in your lawn. To solve this, apply a fungicide and fertilize the land.

20. Small Orange Pustules on Grass Blades in Lawn

Orange pustules and smudgy spots are caused by rust. You can solve this by watering the land to keep it moist and fertilize it. Also, apply fungicide for severe cases. Most frequently mow the land and remove the trimmings.

21. Green Circular Patches in Lawn that Dies

The green patches are known as "fairy rings". These rings sometimes result in mushrooms to form. In solution, apply fertilizer and well aerate your lawn. Try to keep the land wet for about 4 to 5 days.

22. Brown Grass Patches in Late Summer Lawn

The likely cause of these large brown patches of grass is small grubs that are found underneath the brown areas. Dig up some of the soil of these areas and look for these grubs. To solve this, apply Chlorpyrifos, Isofenphos or Diazinon. The ideal time to apply is just after the eggs have been laid. You can also check with a local Cooperative Extension Service or a professional nursery to know the ideal time to take this step.

23. Seasonal Swamp

Implant some water-tolerant plants in low, wet areas to transform it into a rain garden. Use plants, such as perennials and shrubs that can withstand pooling water and also climates of drought. The revised soil and water tolerant plants can absorb the excess water and can slowly permeate into the surface of the earth instead of collecting on the surface of your lawn or flowing into the storm sewer.

24. Proliferating Mushrooms

The sad news about mushrooms is they are almost impossible to get rid of completely. Turf expert Bob Mugaas said that you can pull off the mushrooms at any time. This will temporarily relieve your lawn from mushrooms. However, this is not a permanent solution. By eliminating decaying organic matter and by fitting good quality drainage system, you can make your lawn less comfortable for fungi. Other than that, you should replace dispatch the old mulch, aerate, dig up buried pipes, grind down stubs and rake away grass trimmings.

25. Red Thread

This is one of the most common fungal diseases that your lawn may suffer from. This disease is developed in plants that are highly deficient in nitrogen. The main cause behind the occurrence of red thread is the fungus Laetisaria fuciformis. It kills the grass in rare cases and the patches can be revived with proper lawn treatment and care. The possible symptoms include the grass to develop a reddish shade which later on turns light brown or may look like bleached while the leaves stick together. The size of patches vary, usually ranging from 7.5 to 25 cm (3 to 10 inch) in diameter, or can also be much smaller.

26. Snow Mould or Fusarium Patch

Fusarium Patch, or commonly known as "snow mould", is a typical cause of the brown patches in lawns. It is mostly widespread in autumn season or during the mid of winter. However, they may attack your lawn at any time of the year. The fungus Monographella nivalis is the primary cause of snow mould and they first appear as small patches of yellowish dying grass becoming brown later on. Sometimes small patches merge together to form bigger patches and affect bigger areas. The diameter of the patches may increase in size and reach up to 30 cm (12 inches). Usually during monsoon weather or in wet climates, a pinkish or white cotton-like fungal growth can be noticed, particularly at the border of the patches.

27. Take-all Patch

This is one of the deadliest and most damaging diseases that your lawn can get affected with. Luckily it is not very common and it usually first appears during the mid-summer season. Take-all patch is caused by the fungal action of Gaeumannomyces graminis, which is formerly known as Ophiobolus graminis. In this way, it has the former common name of ophiobolus patch.

Take-all patch first appeared as tiny circular patches having the diameter of about 50 cm to 100 cm (20 inches to 40 inches). This disease has a tendency to affect curved or other fine looking leaf grasses resulting in dying patches of straw-coloured grass. Eventually, the patches disappear after December but can continue to come back again and again for many years.

28. Insects Manifestation

Often insects can take over your beautiful lawn and build their nests. This can be harmful for your lawn and a nuisance, especially if they decide to crawl into you house! Before you lay your hand over an insecticide, you first need to take a closer look and determine which type of insects you are dealing with. Once you know it, you can buy a targeted insecticide that is just made to eliminate that insect.

29. Grass is Growing in Clumps

If grubs are present under the soil, they eat away the roots of lawn grasses and plants. This causes turfs to become weak and clumps of grass peel away by the handful. Grubs are small, fat, white worms that can be killed using grub killer. If ignored, then weak lawn can be easily pulled up like a mat.

30. Grass Becomes Matted

Consecutives nights of wetness can cause fungus to form in your lawn which may turn the color of the grass as matt. Damp, warm and humid environment is the ideal atmosphere for fungi to thrive in. You must examine the blades of the grass closely to identify the issue. If the lawn has dead spots or discoloration, look for fungi in the ring like a spider web. Take experts' help to deal with the problem or just use good quality pesticides.

31. Have a Good Length

Maintain a good measurement of lawn length throughout the year. You should never over-shave or scalp the land as it will make the grass weak.

32. Feed Lawn Well

Make sure you feed your lawn well throughout the year via a lawn feed in summer and in spring. However, in late summer and autumn, you should avoid giving an excess of nitrogen fertilizer. Instead, use autumn lawn feed during this time of the year.

33. Improve Drainage System with Solid-Tine

Improve the drainage system of your lawn by forking the soil or using a solid-tine, or even better, utilizing a hollow-tine aerator in the autumn season. This step is necessary as poor drainage system and water-logged areas will encourage the development of diseases and diminishes the health of the grass.

34. Remove Lawn Thatches

In spring and autumn, scarify the lawn thatches with an electric scarifier or using a spring-tine rake to move away the thatches, moss or other dead organic waste products. Thatch can encourage the development of lawn diseases and so you need to get rid of them and assist your lawn soil in getting well-aerated.

35. Sweep Away Grass Clippings

Dispose the grass trimmings in order to reduce the presence of a fungus, or they might attack your lawn again and re-infect the soil in the lawn.

36. Moisturize the Lawn in Dry Climates

In summer, the grass becomes weak for which the dry lawn can become more prone to diseases. Hence, it is very necessary to water your lawn regularly thoroughly during the prolonged dry climates of summer.

37. Kill Chinch Bugs with Soap Flakes

Chinch bugs eat the lawn grass, removing the sap from the stem and the crown of each grass blade. Grass under attack from cinch bugs will appear as yellow and dies off in patches. Treat these bugs by sprinkling over some soap flakes, pour water to melt it and cover with flannel sheet. The bugs will run and get stuck on the sheet and you can dispose them off.

38. Boric Acid for Clover mites

Clover mites can damage your lawn, as they're voracious feeders of plant tissue. They tend to hide in the bark of plants and trees. They are most active during the summer and so it is better to kill them during this time. Treat these by preparing an insecticides mixing together boric acid with some water. Pour this mixture into a spray bottle and spray it regularly along the entry points being used by mites, or simply sprinkle dry boric acid powder around the infested plant's stem.

39. Glyphosate for Tall Fescue Grass

Tall fescue is a European native which is classified as Festuca arundinacea. These are often unwanted by the residents. You can chemically control them using a glyphosate product like the Roundup. However, Roundup is a non-selective herbicide and this means that it will not discriminate between the grass you wish to keep and the grass you wish to remove.

40. Solarisation to Kill Crabgrass

Crabgrass and other weeds are few of the many invaders that may threaten the health and looks of your lawn, flowerbeds and vegetable gardens. If you want to kill the crabgrass and other weeds, you can try solarisation, where the sun bakes the underlying ground, efficiently killing crabgrass and most annual and perennial weeds. Make the target area moist, cover it with a clear plastic sheet. Keep the edges of the sheet from moving by weighing it down with bricks or rocks. The solarization is complete after five to seven weeks. The process controls the weeds and it can also eradicate other pests and problems, like nematodes and bacteria.

41. Dicamba for Creeping Charlie

You need to understand when dealing with to get rid of creeping charlie plant is that it, like most lawn weeds, thrive best in an unhealthy lawn. In order to wipe away creeping charlie, you should apply dicamba based herbicide to the lawn in early fall when creeping charlie plant is growing most actively. As a result, it will become weak enough so that it will have a difficult time surviving the winter.

42. Controlling Fusarium Wilt Disease

Fusarium blight is a soil-borne pathogen that attacks many types of plants, with ornamental flowers and some vegetables. The fungus also harms plants in the nightshade family, like tomatoes and peppers. Affected plants become wilt and experience other symptoms, like faded, yellowed foliage and stunted growth. Fusarium fungus is most prevalent in warm soils and in old plant debris. The most effective way to prevent infection in your crops or plants is rotation and sterilization. You should never plant the same crop in the same place annually. Sterilize pots with a bleach solution and new soil used when reusing them. Also, kill the fungus by solarizing beds by spreading black plastic over an area in full sun for a month. The extreme high temperatures will burn the fungus and prevent Fusarium from attacking. You should clean tillage equipment, shoes and other tools that might have encountered infected soil. Remove all old plant debris annually, or better, burn it. Never compost contaminated material as this provides an ideal incubation condition for propagating the fungus.

43. Save Lawn from Melting Out

Helminthosporium leaf spot, also known as melting out, will cause large brown areas of dead grass in your lawn. The grass will turn brown, dry up and disappear. Protective methods and reseeding will keep this disease under control. Avoid heavy spring fertilization by fertilizing during fall. Maintain the grass 3 to 4 inches tall. Healthy lawns are more resistant to melting out and other diseases. You can reseed dead regions with a combination of several disease resistant cultivars, like Nugget, Parade, Adelphi, Baron, Eclipse, and Touchdown. You can overseed the lawn to help build in disease resistance to future infections.

44. Grow Grass, Not Moss

Sometimes your lawn may get covered with moss instead of grass. Poor drainage or acid soils will cause a thin lawn and moss. Perform a soil test to determine what type and how much fertilizer is needed. The test will also find out the soil pH and indicates if it needs to be adjusted. Adjust the pH only if required by the soil test. Improper treatment can result in years of additional problems. Try to core aerate the lawn during spring once the grass is actively growing. Then spread a thin layer of compost over the aerated soil surface to improve the soil and your lawn. Overseed the lawn with a grass seed mix suited for shaded areas and wait for the result.

45. Planting below Bird Feeders

Sunflowers are allelopathic plants. These prevent competing plants from growing close by. This is an effective survival mechanism used by buckthorn, black walnuts and some other plants. You should mulch directly under the bird feeder to reduce weeds, conserve the soil and lessen the need to cut the grass around the feeder. Also, you can plant groundcovers and flowers just outside the mulched area. These will creep into the mulched area while the taller flowers will mask the view.

46. Kill Quack Grass

At first ensure it is quack and not crabgrass. Usually in midsummer, crabgrass is first noticed and in the fall it turns purple and dies after dropping thousands of seeds. Crabgrass can be easily controlled through proper care and if needed a pre-emergent applied in spring. Traditional crabgrass pre-emergents are applied when the vanhoutte and lilac flower buds swell. On the other hand, quack grass is a perennial grass weed that is present all season. When you dig out a portion it will have a long white root-like rhizome attachment. Anything that kills quack and other perennial weed grasses will also damage your bluegrass. You can spot treat affected areas with a vegetation killer, like Finale or Roundup during early May or September and reseed.

47. Make your Lawn Rust Free

Your lawn may develop brown spots that may release an orange powdery residue on your shoes. The powder may even get on your dogs paws. The orange residue is from a fungal disease called rust. It is a common issue on newly seeded and drought stressed lawns. The rust symptoms tend to disappear as new lawns mature or drought conditions subside. Usually, fungicide treatments are not needed. Just be patient and reseed any dead places in spring or fall.

48. Remedy against Urine Burn

Urine burns are only a kind of fertilizer burn. You can reduce the damage to the lawn by diluting the salts from the urine. This is done by pouring water over the area where the dog or someone else shitted. It is not too practical to follow the dog everywhere with a sprinkling can. Some commercial products are available in the market. However, nothing is much more effective than water. The same is true for the homemade concoctions. In fact some of these concoctions can cause even more damage. Some owners mulch areas of their landscape around trees and shrubs and potty train their dogs. Mulch is beneficial for the plants and won't be damaged by dog urine.

49. Eco-friendly Treatment against Sod Webworm

The immature worm-like larval stage, i.e. the caterpillar, of the dull colored adult sod webworm causes these problems. They feed on the grass and cause the thinning and the bare patches in the lawn. You can start by maintaining the health of your lawn. Fertilize properly, mow high, and don't leave your trimmings on the lawn. A healthy lawn can fend off this problem and other insects and diseases in a better way. This remedy is enough to manage small populations. Bacillus thuringiensis and neem are effective on the young larvae. The products are sensitive to sunlight and heat, so use them late in the day or early in the evening.

50. Wipe out the Snow Mold

Snow mold in the spring is one effect of a snowy winter. Sometimes a fuzzy gray or pink growth appears over the surface. You should rake these areas lightly to speed drying and stimulate grass growth. During the early May, reseed the places that do not recover from the damage. Encourage healthy growth with fall fertilization, proper watering, and a light raking of places where snow tends to linger late during the spring.

51. Discourage Wild Onions

Wild onion is a stubborn weed to control. It spreads by by seed and by forming underground bulbets. You can keep your lawn healthy and better able to crowd out these and other weeds by proper mowing, watering, and fertilization. Regular mowing prevents seed set and flowering, so additional seedlings won't develop. Unlike other weeds the most suitable time to spray wild onion is just after mowing the lawn. The cut stems absorb the weed killer in a better way. Repeat the process as needed when the plants are growing and recently mowed. Broadleaf weed killers or vegetation killers like Roundup will kill the wild onion in your lawn. You must avoid treating centipede and St Augustine grasses in the spring green up.

Chapter 4 - Environmental Issues

A Huge amount of pesticides and chemical fertilizers are used in every acre of lawn than on an equivalent area of farmland. The continued practice of these products are linked to environmental pollution, increased risk on the health of the local human population, disturbance in the ecosystem of lawn, and other hazards. Other criticism, concerns and issues regarding lawns derive from the consequences of the environment:

- Biodiversity can be negatively affected by lawns, particularly when it is large and covers huge are. Lawns, especially in U.S.A, can consist of introduced species which are not native to a place, and this can make a home for the species, therefore protecting the species.

- Maintenance of lawn requires usage of inorganic fertilizers, herbicides, fungicides and synthetic pesticides and these can damage the environment. According to the estimation of the United States Environmental Protection Agency, every year in the United States approximately 70,000,000 pounds (32,000,000 kg) of harmful pesticide ingredients are poured on suburban lawns.

- The estimation also states that more herbicides are used in one acre of lawn than are utilized by farmers for cultivating crops.
- Countries like Denmark, Sweden, Belize, Kuwait and Norway have imposed restriction laws on the practice of herbicides.
- About 17 million gallons of gasoline have been estimated to be spilled every summer when refuelling the lawn care and garden machines in the United States. This is almost 50% more than that of the spillage in the incident of Exxon Valdez.
- The practice of fertilizers, pesticides and fossil fuels for application, manufacturing and distribution are being held responsible for causing global warming. On the other hand, sustainable organic techniques have been proved to eliminate the effects of global warming.

- **Water conservation:**

  A Large amount of water is required to maintain a luscious green land. It is very common and acceptable in the temperate British Isles. This is the place where the idea of the lawn originated. This is so as natural rainfall is usually sufficient to maintain the health of a lawn. However, during drought hosepipe bans may be banned by the water suppliers.

  An exporting lawn that is perfect for more arid places of the globe, like the U.S, Australia, and Southwest, reduced water resources which were already scarce in those areas. These demands bigger and more environmentally aggressive system of water supply. Normally grass turns inactive during cold, winter months, and becomes brown in dry, hot summer months. This reduces its demand for water. Many people do not like the dead, brown look of the grass, and so continue to water them in the summer months. Grass can be resilient to drought and can recover soon.

- People of the United States use about 50 to 70% of residential water for landscaping; maximum of it goes to lawns. According to the estimation of IA 2005 NASA study on conservatively, almost 128,000 square kilometres (49,000 square mi; 32,000,000 acres) of cultivated lawn in the United States. This is thrice the area of cultivated corn.
- It is true that maintaining a lawn can require using up of precious resources, particularly during extreme climatic conditions. David Ingle Smith observed in 1995 data that under extreme weathers in summer drought times, about 90% of the water used in Canberra, Australia was used in lawns.

- **Chemicals:**

  General citizens become increasingly concerned over the utilization of fertilizer and pesticide and the potential health risks. They also worry about the implementation of legislation, like the Us Food Quality Protection Act in late 20th century, which has been designed to reduce the addition of synthetic chemicals (pesticides) in the lawns of urban landscapes. Due to the health concerns of public over the safety and environmental effect of the pesticides and the chemical fertilizers, the US Environmental Protection Agency and other local governments have decided to ban these harmful lawn care products. These products also cause the death of about 7 billion birds every year which has led to an alarming issue.

- **Reducing environmental effect:**

- Urban smog is increased by lawnmowers run on gasoline in the United States where they are used to maintain lawn heights. The EPA has authorised emission controls on engines in new lawnmowers to reduce smog since 1997 as it was found that lawnmowers run on gasoline made up to 5% of smog in urban areas.

- Carbon sequestration welfares of lawns balanced lawn care inputs and revealed that they might not contribute to anthropogenic global warming, as was shown in 2010 study on lawn care.

- On the other hand with a high net emission of nitrous oxide and carbon dioxide, lawns maintained dexterously with mowing, leaf blowing and irrigation and high fertilization rates have large global warming probability.

- An advantage of a healthy lawn is it prevents runoff and erosion of bare soil and filters contaminants. The negative impact of lawns on the environment can be lowered by using ecological techniques like organic lawn management. Low volume irrigation, low herbs, higher mowing procedures, native grasses, sedges, keeping grass clippings in place as "grasscycling", an integrated pest control system, high-class organic fertilizer and the use of compost, and including a variety of trees, shrubs, perennials, and other plants surrounding the lawn; these are some of the other methods that can be employed.

- Maintenance requirements and pollution can be lowered by integrating a variety of low-maintenance perennials and replacing turf grass with low-maintenance groundcovers while trees and shrubs can replace ordinary lawn spaces; all of this also increases the wildlife and artistic value of the lawn.

Chapter 5 –Lawn Maintenance Tools and Equipments

A garden without a beautiful lawn is like a mermaid without the soul! Lawns cannot beautify themselves. You have to put some effort if you want to enjoy the enchanting view of the luscious green land outside your window. Some essential tools are mentioned in this chapter to care and maintain your garden well.

Lawn Spreader

Now comes the turn of the lawn spreader. This tool is not necessarily essential but is very useful without any doubt. All lawns get benefitted from a feed. The easiest and the quickest way to spread the feed over the land evenly is by using a lawn spreader. Most of the spreaders have adjustable settings so that customers can spread over varieties of products, such as grass seed, lawn sand and triple action products including moss killer, lawn feed, and weed killer. You can choose to spread these products by your hand, however, a spreader will assist you in applying more accurately and evenly and also prevents overdosing your lawn for which the grass can be damaged and patches may form on the ground.

Leaf Rake

You should buy plastic and flexible leaf rake. This tool is particularly helpful in the autumn when you need to pick up dead leaves that fall on the ground. Leaving dead leaves on the lawn not only prevent the grass from getting sunlight but can also decompose to create a sanctuary for the fungus to grow and diseases to develop. The plastic rakes do not spike or poke the leaves and also do not get clogged up so easily, unlike the spring metal lawn rakes. In addition, plastic leaf rakes are gentler towards the grass when you rake the lawn on a regular basis to pick up and remove the leaves.

Scarifier

Scarifier is nothing but a machine that can slice through your lawn and can carry away the pile of thatch. This also aerates (letting in the air) the top soil which is required to rejuvenate an old weary lawn. To get fine and perfect looking lawn, you should scarify the land once in a year or once in two years. Just like most of the other lawn maintenance, autumn or late spring is the ideal times of the year to scarify your lawn.

Lawn Rake

If you want to buy something inexpensive, go for lawn rake. It is one of the cheapest tools for lawn care and maintenance but is very useful. As time will pass, you will have a pile build-up of dead grass (thatch), moss or weeds. This can prevent light and moisture from reaching the live grass and also provide a platform for the growth of suffocating mossy patches and vexatious lawn weeds. You should rake your lawn every once or twice a month. However, you should never rake in frosty or in very cold weather, otherwise, the blades of the grass will be damaged. Make sure you pick up and throw away all the residues you raked up. Manual rakes are very useful in tidying up the lawn, but for larger and more spacious garden, powered lawn rakes are more sensible to buy.

Edging Shears

It feels very good to have a nicely mowed and clipped lawn, but to make it look perfect you need to cut the edges of the lawn neatly. You must cut the edges with using very sharp cutters, or else the grass will tear and the torn edges will turn brown. When you cut the grass, you must hold the cutters in an upright position. This is to avoid poking into the soil and making the edges slanted. However, you need to have patience to do this and every time you edge your lawn, it will gradually become smaller.

Edging Iron

Sometimes edging iron is known as "half-moon" because of its curvy shape. This tool is very useful for smoothing your edges and also for making new shapes or border lines of your lawn. You need to use this tool vertically to slice down just at the edges of the current border in order to sharpen and flatten the edges again. For cutting into new borders, edging iron is ideal for slicing into the turf. All you need to do is to use cut your new border using the edging iron and then move away the unwanted grass using a fork.

Hose

Watering your garden well in dry seasons is very important to keep the lawn green, healthy and lush. Keeping the soil moist also helps in strengthening the roots, so damage in winter is less likely to happen. You should make a common practice to go outside in your lawn and sprinkle over water on the green grass every day. However, this means that the water will only permeate through only a few centimetres of the top soil. In this case, the roots of the grass will flow towards the water and as a result, will grow near the surface of the topsoil. This means that the soil will dry out quickly and be more prone to damage. A nice, prolonged soaking every once or twice a week in dry seasons will make sure a moist environment for your grass and will encourage the growth of deep, strong root network.

Lawn Mowers

Unless you own a flock of sheep, it would probably be a good idea to invest your money in purchasing a good lawn mower. There are thousands of varieties to choose from with different built-in features. For larger and more spacious lawns, it is best to go for petrol mower. Usually, small and medium size lawns can work things out with an electric mower, or alternatively, you can go for the push along mower if you want to burn some calories with a bit of a workout!

Lawn mowers with stripes should be bought which has rollers since clipping the lawn too short will make you unable to see the strips, as well as, encourage the growth of moss and weeds. You can also buy mulching mowers that shear the grass into tiny pieces that are left on the lawn to decompose and feed the lawn.

There are some mowers available in the markets that come with a collection box. These mowers do not clip the grass into fine pieces to be left on the lawn. Therefore, it is best to utilize the collection box to gather the residues, unless you want to rake the lawn after mowing.

Conclusion

The lawn that you can see outside your window is nothing like the weed free, luscious and green yard that you imagine in your dream world. In fact, the yard looks so out of control that you might wonder where to start from! A perfect looking lawn in front of our house gives us a platform to show-off in front of friends. But don't worry. You don't need to give a lot of effort to maintain your lawn. Just by following some simple tips and basic information, you will be able to do the job with ease. The basic needs are quite simple- the sun, water, and fertilized soil. Once your lawn receives these, you are all set.

If You liked this book please rate it on Amazon.com. The author would be really appreciated. Thank You!

26657486R00033

Printed in Great Britain
by Amazon